SURVIVING TERROR

TRUE TEEN STORIES FROM AROUND THE WORLD

True Teen Stories from

IRAQ

Surviving ISIS

Ashley M. Ehman

Cavendish
Square

New York

Published in 2019 by Cavendish Square Publishing, LLC
243 5th Avenue, Suite 136, New York, NY 10016

Library of Congress Cataloging-in-Publication Data

Names: Ehman, Ashley, author.
Title: True teen stories from Iraq : surviving ISIS / Ashley M. Ehman.
Description: First edition. | New York, NY : Cavendish Square Publishing,
LLC, 2019. | Series: Surviving terror: true teen stories from around the
world | Includes bibliographical references and index.
Identifiers: LCCN 2017058918 (print) | LCCN 2018003605 (ebook) | ISBN
9781502635457 (e-Book) | ISBN 9781502635440 (library bound) | ISBN 9781502635464 (pbk.)
Subjects: LCSH: IS (Organization)--Juvenile literature. |
Iraq--History--2003---Juvenile literature. | Teenage
soldiers--Iraq--History--21st century--Juvenile literature. |
Teenagers--Iraq--History--21st century--Juvenile literature. |
Terrorism--Iraq--History--21st century--Juvenile literature.
Classification: LCC HV6433.I722 (ebook) | LCC HV6433.I722 E36 2019 (print) |
DDC 956.7044/3--dc23
LC record available at https://lccn.loc.gov/2017058918

Editorial Director: David McNamara
Editor: Caitlyn Miller
Copy Editor: Rebecca Rohan
Associate Art Director: Amy Greenan
Designer: Christina Shults
Production Coordinator: Karol Szymczuk
Photo Research: J8 Media

The photographs in this book are used by permission and through the courtesy of:
Photo credits: Cover Ton Koene/Alamy Stock Photo; p. 4 C. Sappa/DeAgostini/Getty Images; p. 8
Pavalena/Shutterstock.com; p. 12 Eng Bilal Izaddin/Shutterstock.com; p. 16 Al-Furqan Media/Anadolu
Agency/Getty Images; p. 20 Brendan Smialowski/AFP/Getty Images; p. 24 Khalid Mohammed/AP
Images; p. 27 Ali Yussef/AFP/Getty Images; p. 31 Chris Hondros/Getty Images; p. 33 Safin Hamed/
AFP/Getty Images; p. 34 Aaron Siirila at English Wikipedia/Wikimedia Commons/File:Embassy of
Iraq, Washington, D.C..jpg/CC BY SA 2.5; p. 36 Alamy Stock Photo; p. 40 Quka/Shutterstock.com; p.
46 Sebastian Backhaus/NurPhoto/Getty Images; p. 51, 66 Peter Hermes Furian/Shutterstock.com; p.
58, 82 Ahmad Al-Rubaye/AFP/Getty Images; p. 61 Alain Jocard/AFP/Getty Images; p. 53, 71 Bulent
Kilic/AFP/Getty Images; p. 73 Daniel Leal Olivas Images/Polaris/Newscom; p. 85 Dr. Hammad Nawaf
Farhan/Shutterstock.com; p. 96 Fpolat69/Shutterstock.com; p. 97 Joseph Eid/AFP/Getty Images.

CONTENTS

1 Iraq: From Ancient Roots to a Nation in Peril. 5

2 The Rise of ISIS. 21

3 Teen Recruits. 37

4 The Casualties of ISIS 59

5 Solving Terror in Iraq. 83

Chronology. 98

Glossary 99

Further Information 101

Bibliography. 103

Index. 109

About the Author. 112

The Abbasid Palace, built in the twelfth or thirteenth century, demonstrates the rich history that shaped Iraq into the country it is today.

CHAPTER ONE

IRAQ: FROM ANCIENT ROOTS TO A NATION IN PERIL

To many people outside of Iraq, the nation is synonymous with war and terrorism. Iraq has indeed suffered through wars, revolts, and political crises since its creation as a modern nation in 1920 and its independence from Great Britain in 1932. Throughout the pages of this book, teens tell their stories of how this perpetual strife has shaped their lives.

Yet there's much more to Iraq's history than conflict. Before it became a defined country, what we now know as Iraq served as a cultural center for rich and vibrant empires. The time period known as the Islamic Golden Age, spanning from the eighth century to the thirteenth century, was an era of immense growth for the Iraqi region. It was during this time, in 762 CE, that the city of Baghdad was established. In fact, Baghdad even came to serve as the capital city for the various rulers. In 830 CE, under the Abbasid caliph, the House of Wisdom was erected within the city limits. This massive library served as a home to many important documents, including one of the first works of algebra. Because the House of Wisdom attracted intellectuals from all over the world, Baghdad became a center of learning for nearly four hundred years. While mathematics and science were popular areas of study, proper medical care was also important. Nearing the tenth century, not only did Baghdad offer its citizens access to twenty-four-hour hospitals and pharmacies, but the region was also working toward providing universal health care.

Aside from intellectual advances, Baghdad was also a hub for Persian trading routes. Because it was located between Europe and Asia, the city was used as a meeting point for various exchanges. While outsiders brought such luxuries as ivory, diamonds, and honey, Baghdad merchants made glass, silk, and paper to exchange with foreign entities. Unfortunately, the Islamic Golden Age was brought to an end when invading Mongols burned down the House of Wisdom, destroying all the texts it housed. Tales from the invasion say that the Mongols destroyed so many books, the

Tigris River ran black with ink as the knowledge housed within those texts was simply washed away.

While there are still many technological advancements coming out of Iraq today, ISIS has hindered its advancement, much like the Mongols did almost eight hundred years ago. The growth of ISIS in Iraq has affected the Iraqi economy, politics, and people. Many innocent civilians have had their lives changed forever because of the direct and indirect effects of ISIS. With 58 percent of the population falling under the age of twenty-four, many young people are exposed to the violence of the Islamic State on a daily basis. To truly understand the hardships these teens face, we must first understand some basic facts about the nation itself.

The Republic of Iraq

Iraq shares borders with Turkey, Syria, Saudi Arabia, Kuwait, Jordan, and Iran. Even though nearly all of its outlying land borders other countries, Iraq is strategically placed so that it maintains a small port with access to the Persian Gulf. It has not always been this way, however. Following the Second World War, there were tensions between Iraq and the Kurdish minority, as well as with Israel. The Jewish state of Israel was established on May 14, 1948, as a direct result of Great Britain relinquishing control of Palestine. Because Iraq and other countries in the region did not recognize Israel as its

Iraq borders six countries. The nation's capital is Baghdad.

own country, they invaded on May 15 of the same year. The invasion contributed to a lack of defined borders for Iraq. Because Iraqis believed the area occupied by Israel belonged to them, the country of Iraq was depicted to be bigger than it actually was on maps. The fight ended in March 1949, after Israel had increased its overall landmass, thus creating an even greater area in which to establish a unified country.

Following the complications with Israel, 1961 brought on a whole new slew of problems. The Kurdish minority group that lived predominantly in Northern Iraq began to believe that they deserved to stand as their own country. In order to do so, they would need to be granted land from the Iraqi government, to which the Kurds felt they had a legitimate right. Following a military coup in 1968, the Kurds aligned with newly established leader Ahmad Hasan al-Bakr and developed the Kurdish Democratic party. As al-Bakr continued through his time in office, it became increasingly clear that he would not grant the Kurds their autonomy.

In spring of 1974, fights broke out between government militants and the Kurdish army. The Kurds were quickly overpowered and forced to live in villages that were lined with barbed wire, following the destruction of their original homes. At that time, the border of Iraq became what it is today.

Despite the complicated history, the land found within its borders makes Iraq a fascinating place. If you imagine blistering heat and desert in Iraq, you're correct. Iraq's climate is that of a typical desert environment. Temperatures can rise above 100 degrees Fahrenheit (37.8 degrees Celsius) during the summer and plummet below 40°F (4.4°C) at night. Rain is scarce during the hotter months; nearly all of Iraq's precipitation falls between the months of December through March.

The landscape of most of Iraq consists of broad plains. In the north, however, there are mountains near the border shared with Turkey. There are also instances of marshy lowlands that even flood during the winter months. As for size, Iraq is just over 438,000 square feet (40,691.5 square meters) in area, making it the sixtieth-largest country in the world. To put that in perspective, Iraq is roughly the same size as three New York States.

The Government and Economy of Iraq

While Iraq's government has taken many forms over its extensive history, it is currently a federal parliamentary representative democratic republic. This means that the country is run by an executive authority. Once elected, this person appoints individuals to serve in his cabinet and other parts of the government. These appointees are known as the Council of Ministers. Like the United States, Iraq's government is organized into three branches: federal, judicial, and legislative. The judicial branch determines court cases using a mix of civil and Islamic law.

Being that Iraq is one of the oil states of the Middle East, it is unsurprising that the vast majority of the country's income comes from producing and exporting crude oil. Oil accounts for 90 percent of government earnings, as well as 80 percent of foreign exchange earnings. ("Foreign exchange earnings" is the term used to describe money brought in through trade with other countries). As suggested by these earnings, crude oil represents 99 percent of Iraq's exports, with the remaining 1 percent belonging to fuels, food, and live animals. In exchange for its exports, Iraq imports food, medicines, and manufactured goods. Even with the presence of oil and the economic benefits it brings, Iraq was still faced with an unemployment rate of 16 percent as of 2015. The high unemployment rate—one of the highest in the world—is due to corruption and a lack of reform in the public sector. Because of these factors, it is extremely difficult for citizens to start their own businesses or secure jobs that pay a living wage. It is also a reason that terrorism has found a foothold in Iraq.

The People of Iraq

Iraq is currently home to an estimated 39,192,111 people, making it the thirty-fifth most populous country in the world. Three-quarters of its population is made up of people of Arabian descent, with the majority of the remainder made up of Kurdish people. As its dominant ethnic group may suggest, the most spoken language in Iraq is Arabic. A staggering 99 percent of Iraq's citizens are Muslim. This figure breaks down into 55 percent Shiite Muslims, while the other 40 percent are Sunni.

Iraq has a dwindling elderly presence; 93 percent of its citizens are fifty-four years old or younger. This could be due to the multiple exoduses Iraq has seen in its recent history.

ISIS can have lasting effects on Iraqi children like these, who were torn from their homes and forced into refugee camps in the wake of violence.

Many of these exoduses are the direct result of ISIS activity, since innocent civilians are only left with the option of leaving their homes if they hope to survive.

These statistics show a country not unlike many others in the Middle East. Facts and figures don't account for why Iraq makes its way into headlines on a regular basis. That's where ISIS comes in.

What Is ISIS?

With beginnings tracing back to 2004, the Islamic State of Iraq and Syria (ISIS), is a fairly young terrorist organization. Also called the Islamic State of Levant, Daesh, or simply the Islamic State, the group was originally founded on the ideas of a Jordanian man named Abu Musab al-Zarqawi. Al-Zarqawi was a former associate of al-Qaeda, a terrorist group that situated itself in Iraq in the late 1980s. Some argue that ISIS is simply a restructuring of the old al-Qaeda group, based on the fact that both militant groups align themselves with anti-Western ideas. Both groups also share the ultimate goal of recognizing the establishment of an independent Islamic state in the Middle East. However, others argue that the two groups are not connected, since ISIS has proved to be much more brutal and more successful in the seizure of various lands throughout Iraq and Syria. As of 2016, it was estimated that ISIS had between twenty thousand and twenty-five thousand militants fighting for their cause. These individuals were fighting in areas of Iraq, Syria, and Libya, with localized attacks in cities in Europe and elsewhere.

Of course, it takes considerable sums of money in order for a terrorist group to thrive. Once described as "the best-funded terrorist organization the US has ever confronted" by David Cohen, the Treasury Department's Undersecretary for Terrorism and Financial Intelligence, ISIS has many different channels of income. First and foremost, the group taps into the energy industry by selling the crude oil from the lands they control. In addition to oil, ISIS takes control of bank accounts and extorts local citizens for more funds. Beyond that, ISIS is known to have private donors who support their cause, stemming from royal families and well-to-do business tycoons. Finally, ransoms have proved to be a source of monetary gain. In fact, ISIS has a reputation for kidnapping people. Through ransoms, bribe money, oil sales, and more, ISIS has established a strong economic foundation.

Stopping ISIS

Unlike terrorist groups of the past, ISIS has proved to be long-lasting and successful in their efforts to recruit and dominate the Middle East. Their violent actions have had repercussions for countries all over the world, making both global and local efforts to dismantle the group a top priority.

Possibly the most obvious way to stop ISIS is the use of military force. One such example of this is the Global Coalition Against ISIS, or the Global Coalition Against Daesh. Currently made up of seventy-three partners, the coalition includes Australia, the United States, Bahrain, and many other countries in regions around the world. As it stands, the coalition has helped local military members reclaim all of ISIS-controlled towns in Iraq. (ISIS still controls some remote territory near Syria.) With a stronger military presence in the area, ISIS members are unable to move about the country freely, making the retrieval of supplies, tactical missions, and recruitment efforts harder to accomplish.

While the tactical use of force is important, there are many nonviolent ways to combat ISIS. The Global Coalition also has a hand in these efforts. One of the most important things to do after retrieving areas from ISIS control is to stabilize the local infrastructure. If a reclaimed city was left to its own devices, only chaos would ensue, making it the perfect target for ISIS to strike yet again. The coalition uses its resources to rebuild schools, educate local law enforcement, and provide development opportunities to the citizens. In doing so, cities are better able to defend themselves and encourage civilians to return to their homes.

Lastly, educating people around the globe proves beneficial to anti-ISIS efforts. Because ISIS is considered to be a radical Muslim group, people can mistakenly believe that all Muslims share ISIS's values and goals. This is grossly inaccurate, as radicalized individuals interpret religious readings differently and attempt to eradicate other religions entirely. The majority of Muslims do not share the same beliefs as those in ISIS do, and the sooner people are educated on the Muslim religion, the sooner the ignorance and hatred surrounding Islamic communities can be stopped. By stopping these prejudiced attitudes, Muslims will feel less isolated and misunderstood. In turn, this will lessen the number of Muslims who join ISIS, since many often join in order to feel a sense of belonging among other Muslims.

ABU BAKR AL-BAGHDADI

Amidst reports of his death in a US airstrike, a man named Abu Bakr al-Baghdadi is still being called the leader of ISIS. While not a lot is known about his past, it is believed that he was born in 1971 in Samarra, a city found north of Baghdad, to a lower–middle class Sunni Muslim family. While he was growing up, Baghdadi was devoutly religious and enjoyed Quranic recitations. This interest in religion continued into his young adult life, as he pursued a degree in Islamic Studies from the University of Baghdad in 1996. He completed his master's degree in 1999 and a PhD in 2007 in the same subject area. Before the United States' invasion of Iraq, reports say Baghdadi served as a cleric at a local mosque. He was first connected with a terrorist group upon the rise of al-Qaeda.

Experts believe Abu Bakr al-Baghdadi continues to lead ISIS.

From there, he connected with ultraconservatives within the group and was later imprisoned for ten months by United States forces. During his time in prison, Baghdadi sharpened his ability to connect groups that were formerly enemies. This talent later allowed him to move up within the ranks to where he is today, as leader of ISIS. Currently, not much is known about his location or even whether he's alive. Despite reports of Baghdadi's death, local officials are unable to provide any confirming details. With the release of a new audiotape in September 2017, there is even more confusion surrounding his fate. In the tape, a voice that sounds like Baghdadi speaks of North Korea and its threats to the United States. According to Ryan Dillon, a spokesman for US forces fighting ISIS, "without verifiable evidence of his death, we have continued to assume that he is alive."

ISIS and the Iraqi People

ISIS grows from a place of power and control, and their presence invokes fear and unrest in the civilians of Iraq. For those that refuse to support their cause, many face abuse and death. As nineteen-year-old Amsha Ali, who was forced to marry an ISIS member, recalls:

> *By God, when they took girls and women it was a very sad feeling for me. I saw a lot of murders, murders of Yazidis, but the killing was not the hardest thing for me. Even when [ISIS] forced my husband, brother-in-law, and my father-in-law on the ground to be murdered—it was painful, but marrying [them] was the worst. It was hardest thing for me.*

Luckily for Ali, and her infant son, she was able to escape. However, Ali still has no idea where her sisters ended up, or even if they are alive. Ali's case is not unique, however. Many innocent people face the brutality of ISIS on a daily basis. With a regular repertoire of killing, kidnapping, and extortion, ISIS has been able to amass power. The history of the group sheds light on how strategy and luck built ISIS.

THE ANTITERRORISM ASSISTANCE PROGRAM

There are many different programs and organizations in place to combat terrorism across the globe. One such program is the Antiterrorism Assistance Program (ATA). Administered by the Office of Antiterrorism Assistance (part of the US Department of State), the ATA is in place to help US allies carry out antiterror initiatives. These initiatives include training civilian security and law enforcement individuals.

The ATA helps developing countries, which are often easy targets for terrorist organizations. These countries usually lack the manpower and resources to put reliable security measures in place. India, Pakistan, Iraq, and Libya are among the countries who have received assistance in the past few years. In Lebanon, the ATA helped modernize and stabilize newly developed security forces. In India, the ATA used their resources to further develop human rights and border security efforts. The ATA addresses weaknesses that need to be resolved and then trains countries accordingly. Beyond that, the program strives to protect national borders, fix and improve upon critical infrastructure flaws, and protect the leaders involved in these efforts. In addition to these goals, the ATA provides assistance in the aftermath of terrorist attacks and manages the response to large-scale threats.

The city of Baghdad has long been a target for terrorists. Al-Qaeda suicide bombers attacked Harthiya Square (shown here) in 2007. Al-Qaeda gave rise to ISIS.

CHAPTER TWO

THE RISE OF ISIS

The Islamic State did not appear overnight. A few key events needed to happen in order for ISIS to take hold. ISIS then learned how to wield influence over the entire world and rose to be one of the most powerful terrorist groups of our time. Throughout its history, ISIS has been the product and the maker of war, political turmoil, and fear.

The Influence of al-Qaeda

While it may seem like ISIS started independently, its beginnings can be traced back to its predecessor, the terrorist group known as al-Qaeda. Formed in 1989, al-Qaeda was an initial blueprint for what would become known as ISIS.

Al-Qaeda's leader, Osama bin Laden, came from a wealthy Saudi Arabian family that specialized in construction projects. This knowledge, and subsequent equipment from the construction industry, helped bin Laden support his followers' guerrilla war tactics. Initially, al-Qaeda was made up of "holy warriors" who had pledged to fight against the Soviet Union's presence in Afghanistan.

That all changed on August 7, 1990. On that day, the United States deployed troops to Saudi Arabia in an attempt to make headway during the Gulf War. It was the United States' intent to set up a base closer to Iraqi leader Saddam Hussein's troops. This strategic move was meant to give the United States a better chance to end the Gulf War. While the strategy did help bring the Gulf War to an end, US presence in Saudi Arabia angered bin Laden. His anger stemmed from American troops' position between Muslim holy sites, including Medina and Mecca. He declared the United States an enemy.

By the time nine years had passed, al-Qaeda had grown in influence and numbers. Multiple attacks around the world were linked to the group. Osama bin Laden was even placed on the FBI's Top Ten Most Wanted list. While bin Laden was now on the global radar, another man, Abu Musab al-Zarqawi, was just beginning his ascent to power through terrorism.

Much like bin Laden, Zarqawi had also sought to fight against the Soviet Union in the late 1980s. Upon his arrival in Afghanistan, however, the war was near completion. In the years that followed, Zarqawi was arrested in Jordan and placed in prison. In fact, he spent the entirety of 1992 until 1998 there, where he was believed to have adopted an extremist following of Islam. In 1999, he returned to Afghanistan.

Once Zarqawi arrived on Afghan soil, the roots of ISIS began to take hold. It was Zarqawi's intent to make contact with the leaders of al-Qaeda and begin gathering the necessary resources for his mission. At the time, Zarqawi was determined to bring revolution to the Fertile Crescent, the area found in the eastern Mediterranean that then stretched through Iraq. At first, Osama bin Laden's men had Zarqawi followed to ensure that he posed no threat to their organization. Once they determined that Zarqawi shared similar views to their own, al-Qaeda leaders met with him. Upon contact, it was clear that Zarqawi had a very simple goal in mind: to bring Sunni Islam back to "the reality of human life." However, Zarqawi lacked the detailed plans to make his vision a reality.

Zarqawi and bin Laden did not combine their groups, but they did align their missions. That said, al-Qaeda and ISIS do not share all the same views. For example, it is thought that bin Laden did not share the same hatred for

Suspected ISIS members are detained for questioning in Ramadi in 2016.

Shiite Muslims that Zarqawi did. However, both shared the ideal that American "infidels" deserved to be killed. Because of this, they formed an alliance centered on the mission at hand—dispelling Americans from their region and growing the Islamic state—but not centered on their own religious beliefs. As a way to help the inexperienced Zarqawi, al-Qaeda leaders gave him a loan to form a military training camp in Afghanistan. This camp was used to attract like-minded individuals who were ready to fight. People prepared to fight for a radical version of Islam are called jihadists.

Zarqawi Pledges Allegiance

Al-Qaeda's hopes to establish an Islamic state were dashed in 2001. After the United States' invasion of Afghanistan and the fall of the Taliban, al-Qaeda's remaining members decamped to different parts of the Middle East. For Zarqawi, the invasion proved to be incredibly beneficial. Not only did the unseating of al-Qaeda leave a void in the region, it also made Iraq the ideal location to form his new group. Zarqawi had predicted that the United States would eventually invade Iraq in order to overthrow the regime that had taken over. By ensuring that he was ready for the invasion, Zarqawi could prove to the Western world and fellow radical Muslims that he was a force to be reckoned with. He recruited followers in 2002 and the beginning of 2003. When the United States sent forces to Iraq in March 2003, Zarqawi's forces were armed and ready. They were successful in bombing the Jordanian embassy and the United Nations headquarters in Baghdad. Beyond that, Zarqawi's hatred for the Shia Islam sect fueled other attacks. He bombed the mosque of Imam Ali, a holy site for Shia Islam, killing more than ninety people.

Burning hatred of Shia Islam affected nearly every aspect of Zarqawi's life. When it came time for him to send in his membership request to al-Qaeda, he failed to mention much that aligned with their goals. It was obvious that he had lost sight of his original political aims. Zarqawi did discuss how he would attract Sunni jihadists and rid Iraq of foreign militant presence. Zarqawi believed that Shiite Muslims were the direct result of the Antichrist, and he sought to eradicate them.

Again, al-Qaeda does not share this view. Therefore, when Zarqawi asked to join his group, bin Laden hesitated. It was the goal of al-Qaeda to rid the Middle East of American military presence. In order to do this, al-Qaeda needed Muslim supporters of all sects in order to foster resentment against the United States. This could not be done if a religious civil war was ignited between Sunni and Shiite Muslims. In 2004, however, Zarqawi ultimately pledged allegiance to al-Qaeda. Zarqawi's new group became known as al-Qaeda in Iraq (AQI). Until 2006, the two groups worked together to wreak havoc in the Middle East.

The Split Begins

After nearly two years of exchanging gunfire and bombing American militants, Abu Musab al-Zarqawi was killed in a United States air strike on June 7, 2006. Following his death, Abu Ayyub al-Masri took his place as leader of al-Qaeda in Iraq. While they gave the impression that it was business as usual, AQI and Masri had other things in mind. On October 15 of that year, AQI fulfilled Zarqawi's goal of establishing an Islamic State in Iraq. They named Abu Omar al-Baghdadi as its leader and "commander of the faithful." The decision was carried out abruptly and did not follow the agreed-upon plan that had been in place between Zarqawi and bin Laden. That plan said they would wait to announce the Islamic State until after American presence had been diminished and they had a stronger Sunni following.

The confusion that ensued had a detrimental effect on the establishment of the Islamic State. Al-Qaeda leaders were taken aback by how little involvement they had in the decision. Globally, people did not understand if this new state was considered part of al-Qaeda or was completely independent. In addition, the announcement made it seem like the alliance between the two groups had ended—al-Qaeda failed to make an announcement of their own, after all. Individuals who had already pledged their allegiance to al-Qaeda leaders were not sure about their loyalties. Should they support Baghdadi? Or should they support the original caliphate, the "commander of the faithful?" Or the

Foreign forces, such as this American soldier, have become a common sight in Iraq as governments around the world fight ISIS.

proclaimed leader of the Islamic State? In the months that followed, Baghdadi worked to make it seem like al-Qaeda was a member of the Islamic State. However, the Islamic State was not meant to serve as a terrorist group and was itself a separate entity.

Unintended Consequences

The premature announcement of the Islamic State in Iraq actually slowed the progress Baghdadi sought to make. ISIS's lack of preparation allowed United States troops to establish a greater presence in Iraq the following year. This led to the disbanding of some ISIS troops and the killing of multiple ISIS members, with the organization maintaining only a fraction of its resources and of its leaders. By 2008, nearly ten thousand of the original fifteen thousand members of ISIS had either been killed or imprisoned. Recruitment during this time was also at an all-time low. Monthly recruits dropped from one hundred twenty individuals to less than ten per month. Had things kept going so poorly, perhaps ISIS would have ceased to exist. Despite overwhelming odds, Baghdadi and his followers caught a break in 2009.

It was during this tumultuous time that the Iraqi Prime Minister, Nouri al-Maliki, began voicing negative opinions about his Sunni peers and fellow leaders. Because of this, Sunnis under his governance began to look toward leaders who adhered to their own beliefs. One such leader was Baghdadi. Maliki's actions positively influenced support for ISIS, and recruitment efforts began to prove more fruitful. While things appeared to be moving in the right direction for the Islamic State, both of its establishing leaders met their demise shortly after. In April 2010, Abu Omar al-Baghdadi and Abu Ayyub al-Masri were killed by US and Iraqi military forces. The two men were succeeded by Abu Bakr al-Baghdadi.

Al-Qaeda Cuts Ties

While they initially put up a cohesive front, al-Qaeda officially cut ties with ISIS on February 3, 2014. This dissociation revealed the level of disconnect that had been happening behind closed doors. It became public knowledge that al-Qaeda was not aware of the creation of the Islamic State when ISIS announced it back in 2006. It seems that al-Qaeda's leadership merely put up a united front to hide internal weaknesses that plagued the two organizations. In the formal announcement issuing the separation, an al-Qaeda commander said, "[ISIS] is not a branch of the al-Qaeda group ... does not have an organizational relationship with it and [al-Qaeda] is not the group responsible for their actions." At one point, al-Qaeda even referred to ISIS as their "problem child." ISIS no longer followed orders given by al-Qaeda leader, Ayman al-Zawahiri, and stated that they "choose the rule of God" over that of Zawahiri. (Al-Qaeda leader Osama bin Laden was killed by US forces in 2011 and was succeeded by Ayman al-Zawahiri.) After the separation between the

SADIYA'S STORY

While many teenagers around the world return home from school with worries about their homework and friends, daily life in Iraq can involve life-or-death concerns too. A girl named Sadiya was fifteen years old at the peak of ISIS's occupation of Iraq. For Sadiya, going to school meant putting herself in danger. Simply living in the city of Mosul meant danger. In a diary entry from October 19, 2004, Sadiya wrote:

> I had a very bad day today. First, when we went to school we heard the sound of bombing nearby and I didn't do well in my exam. In the sixth lesson, we heard another bomb. My dad was near it but thank God he is ok.

Not only was her daily life affected by ISIS and the war, so was Sadiya's outlook on life. As she explains in a diary entry titled, "Can life get worse?": "I am sure that none of you could live one day in Iraq. In Iraq now there is no happy word in our dictionary." At the beginning of the new millennium, teenagers in Iraq questioned their future or even whether their family members would make it home each day.

A bomb destroyed this Baghdad restaurant in 2004.

Beyond the bombings and constant presence of death, Sadiya's diary describes interests held by most teenagers. She had a room to herself, which she saw as a means of self-expression. As she explains, "I love to decorate my room with bears and the things I love because it brings me back my memories." She had fights with her sister and cleaned up the house for her mother. The only thing that made her different from teens in the rest of the world was terrorism's direct impact on her upbringing.

two terrorist groups, al-Qaeda fell into the background. They were no longer relevant or as powerful as their more aggressive counterpart.

The Current State of ISIS

From 2010 up until today, ISIS has continued to thrive. They have been met with counterterrorism strikes and military campaigns many times, but they often prove successful in their endeavors to expand the territory they control. Strategic locations like Tikrit, the Mosul Dam, and Ramadi were all subject to ISIS control at one point or another. Many other places across Iraq and Syria have fallen victim to ISIS militants as well. The United States, France, and various other countries are working with Iraqi military units to combat ISIS.

Beyond expanding their territory in the quest to create a physical Islamic State, ISIS has also been known to carry out global attacks in order to inspire fear. Many individuals, including foreign aid workers and journalists, have been captured and then executed on camera by ISIS militants. Videos of executions are then released for victims' families, countries, and the world to see. In addition to cultivating fear, it is ISIS's hope to inspire like-minded individuals to commit their own acts of terrorism.

The Mosul Dam has been a target for ISIS militants, based on its strategic location and the ability to control civilians by limiting water resources.

Weakened, but Still Influential

Military forces from many countries work together to stop the expansion of ISIS. They also keep track of the groups' movements and target areas where key leaders may be hiding out. Once an area is identified, it is then subject to airstrikes and strategic force. Bringing down the leadership of a terrorist organization can lead to the demise of the organization as a whole. A prime example is the fight against al-Qaeda. May 1, 2011, tipped the fight in America's favor. After United States forces located Osama bin Laden's compound in Pakistan, they executed him. After bin Laden's death, al-Qaeda saw a steep decline.

There are signs that ISIS is weakening, such as the loss of the majority of their territory in Iraq since their peak. However, ISIS is still able to draw in recruits thanks to the deceptive ways they target young people, as well as the benefits they claim to offer.

"THAT'S EVERY DAY
... IN IRAQ"

There are many teens in the region facing scarring situations. In 2014, a teen named Sarah was given the opportunity to compare American living to what she experienced in her home of Baghdad. While on a trip to Cleveland, Ohio, as part of an American and Iraqi embassy trip, she and her fellow peers detailed what they went through on a daily basis. As Zach Schwartz, a Vice.com writer recalled, "They showed me

Officials at the Iraqi Embassy in DC sponsor trips abroad for young Iraqis so that they can share their perspectives and gain new experiences.

pictures they had taken on their iPhones of dead bodies laying on the streets of Iraq. 'You think that's bad?' they said, almost boasting. 'That's every day ... in Iraq.'" In another exchange, upon entering a coffee shop, Sarah said, "I love coffee shops! Except you can't go to them in Baghdad because they get bombed all the time." Aside from bombings, the people in her life are also continually affected. Sarah's uncle was killed by ISIS. She explains that nearly everyone in Iraq has lost someone to ISIS. On her street alone, twenty-eight women have been kidnapped by militants. Interestingly, though, she does not feel sorry for herself.

As her visit to the United States came to an end, it was the American people that she was feeling sorry for. For Sarah, she "always imagined America to be a land of dreams and opportunity," but her tour of the country had changed that impression. "People here seem very depressed." For someone coming from a country riddled by bombs and death around every corner, this may be a surprising thing to hear. As she puts it, "one thing I love about Iraqis is that they still have hope. And they love life. And even though there are bombings happening all the time ... you live while you can. And if you die, you die. And so they go and live a normal, happy life, but with that in mind."

ISIS propaganda is designed to portray the group as a powerful military force.

CHAPTER THREE

TEEN RECRUITS

ISIS is a brutal organization responsible for rape, torture, and murder. They claim to follow Islam but in reality do no such thing. While it seems obvious to most people that ISIS is not an organization to engage with, the group still uses several recruitment techniques successfully. These means of recruitment are vital to their continued existence, and because they see teenagers as vulnerable, teen recruits factor heavily into ISIS's strategy.

Recruitment Tactics

Unlike terrorist groups of the past, ISIS has a valuable tool at its disposal: the internet. The World Wide Web allows ISIS to connect with people on a global scale, targeting individuals that are most likely to join their efforts. Like mainstream advertisers, ISIS uses proven methods to attract different demographics to their content. This content is then meant to shape the viewer's way of thinking and paints the Islamic State in a desirable light.

Social media is ISIS's most effective online tool. The use of social media is especially important to attracting younger people to their cause. As one study from 2014 showed, 89 percent of eighteen- to twenty-nine-year-olds had at least one account on a social media platform. Now ISIS is leveraging that statistic. In 2015 alone, it was documented that some ninety thousand pro-ISIS posts were made across a variety of social media websites. This number may have even been larger, but not all posts were visible to researchers.

While ISIS-driven posts can be found across the internet, one of the most popular platforms that the group uses is Twitter. The microblogging site allows the organization to access a plethora of potential recruits. This reach is due to Twitter's fast and easy distribution of content. At the beginning of 2015, there was in excess of forty-six thousand ISIS-related Twitter accounts.

Recruitment efforts go far beyond just tweeting on a regular basis, however. Because tweets are a passive form of communication, recruiters have to enlist other tactics to garner support and radicalize their followers. One tactic that they rely heavily on is grooming. Grooming means influencing an individual to see things through another, often distorted, view of the world. This approach works to attract people to the Middle East to fight with the jihadists, as well as carry out lone-wolf attacks in the name of ISIS on foreign soil.

Social Media Recruitment: Step-by-Step

In order to successfully groom an individual who could become a new recruit, ISIS follows a set of steps to promote the lifestyle and mission they are fighting for. It all starts with first contact. Initial contact is made by either the recruiter or the individual themselves. Recruiters are always looking for people that are sympathetic to their cause, and they make themselves readily available to those who seek them out for more information.

The next step ISIS takes is to create a small, tight-knit community around the individual. Recruiters ensure that they are available at all times of the day. This tactic goes beyond just being prepared for direct messages. Islamic State recruiters also maintain an active online presence, with the average recruiter tweeting fifty times daily. Some even tweet upwards of 240 times a day! This allows their followers any number of opportunities to interact with the content they

TECHNOLOGY AND RECRUITMENT

SIS is hardly the first terrorist group to exist, of course. There have been the likes of al-Qaeda, Boko Haram, and the Haqqani Network. Terrorist groups stretching back farther in history had no means of conducting long-distance recruitment. Before the dawn of technology, the vast majority of terrorist groups relied on word of mouth. This, in combination with the distribution

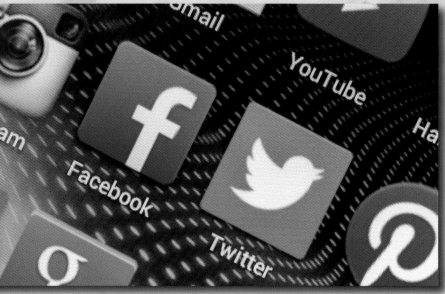

Social media helps ISIS with recruitment efforts and the spread of propaganda.

of propaganda pieces, was often what drew people to these groups. Because of their relatively small scope of influence, terrorist organizations that existed prior to the internet were often localized to one area and rarely spread much farther than their own country.

Even after the internet took off, terrorist groups like al-Qaeda still faced some difficulties communicating their message to potential recruits. They were still stuck in the era before social media could be used as a tool. That did not stop them from becoming household names, however. There was plenty of news coverage and stories written about terrorist groups and their attacks. This coverage allowed their reach to expand beyond the Middle East but still caused some problems internally. Terrorist groups were not controlling the message that was being distributed.

That all changed when ISIS was formed in the midst of the social media boom. By determining their target audience and marketing themselves accordingly on sites like Facebook and Twitter, ISIS has been very successful at shaping their own image and message.

are sharing. It also influences how the recruiters are perceived and can be seen to have a humanizing effect—not everything recruiters share is directly related to ISIS. Sometimes they share pictures or posts they find interesting or amusing as well. Once the individual seems actively connected to the Islamic State community, recruiters begin to influence them to disconnect from people who do not share ISIS's views. By ensuring that the person is isolated, recruiters know the individual becomes more likely to seek out ISIS-related activities. Encouraging the target to disassociate from non-Muslim people is just the beginning. Recruiters then go further still and asks that the recruit not communicate with Muslims who have mainstream views. As a result of this more open support for the Islamic State, recruits' social media accounts are often suspended. Suspension works in the terrorist group's favor, however. The recruits often rejoin the social media platform by creating a different account. In order to avoid suspension in the future, the recruit follows fewer people in new account, so as to avoid being reported. In turn, this further promotes the isolation tactic that ISIS uses to influence its new followers.

Once a relationship has been developed, communications tend to move to private mediums. Popular choices for messaging are Kik, WhatsApp, and Telegram due to the encryption and extra security measures those platforms have in place. In addition to online communications, recruiters often supplement these private messages with physical mailings. After establishing these lines of communication, the recruiters will begin asking for action to take place. Requests are made tactfully, as the recruiter knows that only certain individuals will do certain things. Therefore, recruiters are quick to suggest acts that they know that individual would be comfortable performing. Recruiters often base requests on how radicalized the recruit has become. A call to action could range from traveling to the Middle East and other ISIS-controlled areas, carrying out terrorist attacks on home soil, or participating in social media activism.

Beyond Twitter, ISIS's social media presence expands to other popular sites like Tumblr and Facebook. These sites make efforts to limit the amount of content that is put out by ISIS, for obvious reasons. A large number of ISIS posts break the user terms and agreements of social media sites. Based on Twitter's guidelines, for example, anything that promotes violence or threats or encourages unlawful behavior will result in a suspended account. Because of these suspensions, the CEOs of both Twitter and Facebook have received death threats from ISIS members.

As can be seen, ISIS and its recruiters are extremely savvy on social media. Their savvy allows them to connect with their potential recruits and portray themselves in a desirable light. Young Westerners are a prime target in these recruitment efforts. ISIS's strategy seems to be working, as many young people have made or attempted the journey to ISIS-controlled areas. It all comes down to the lies recruiters tell.

The Thrall of ISIS

To most people, the thought of joining a terrorist group is unimaginable. However in 2014, nearly two thousand Western teenagers left their home countries to join the ranks of ISIS. They were motivated by the perceived benefits that the group has to offer.

First, ISIS uses jihadist propaganda to its advantage. These are materials that support the organization's messages in a way that makes their acts of terrorism seem cool and mainstream. In one example, ISIS released what looked like a cover of the popular video game *Call of Duty*. However, this fake edition of the game read "Call of Jihad" and had other radicalized Muslim references on it. It is materials like this that draw in young men, as they are often the audience for these games. One British teenager even explained his experience as a jihadist as "better than that game *Call of Duty*." By making acts of terrorism seem like a video game, time spent in ISIS is perceived as fun by those on the outside looking in. ISIS even has a staff of experienced video makers and designers

ANONYMOUS VS. ISIS

While much of the fight against ISIS takes place on foreign soil in military confrontations, there are still those who are attempting to fight behind the scenes. The group known as Anonymous is doing just that. Represented by the Guy Fawkes mask, this group of hacktivists is doing their part to cripple the terrorist organization. Having realized that ISIS recruitment largely functions on social media, Anonymous began hacking into ISIS-run Twitter accounts.

They didn't stop at simply hacking into their accounts, however. Following the Orlando shooting at Pulse nightclub, members of Anonymous filled ISIS-run Twitter accounts with gay pride posts and the rainbow flag. Irate ISIS members bombarded Anonymous with death threats. However, Anonymous did not back down. The Anonymous Twitter account even tweeted, "Anonymous from all over the world will hunt you down. You should know that we will find you and we will not let you go." They then followed up with another tweet, reading, "We will launch the biggest operation ever against you. Expect massive cyber attacks. War is declared. Get prepared." Anonymous's anti-ISIS strategy has also included doxing email addresses, taking down ISIS-related websites, and having Twitter accounts removed.

on hand to continually pump out interesting content for their social media accounts. This content ranges from home–movie quality videos to executions and bombings that have been edited to look like scenes from a feature film. In order to attract more members, ISIS has also employed various references from the Western world to appeal to people in those regions. Some of these materials make nods to *Saw*,

An ISIS propaganda magazine

V for Vendetta, and other gory movies. By varying their techniques, they can target different audiences and reach a broader swath of people.

Another aspect of ISIS's appeal is the idea that there is a religious obligation to join the group. ISIS's association with the religion of Islam makes some Muslims feel it is their duty to serve in the organization. In addition, ISIS and its mission are focused on an idealized and "perfect" Muslim state. They give the impression that they are fighting for a religious utopia and claim they only seek to return Islamic beliefs back to the right and sound ways asked of them by their God. The propaganda they distribute furthers this idea by showcasing a perfect world filled with happy children, plentiful markets, and nice communities. They claim this utopia is only possible if other religions are eradicated. Therefore, ISIS says that in order to be a good Muslim, one must make sacrifices and join the Islamic State.

Another reason ISIS appeals to a younger demographic is that by taking part in ISIS's activities, teenagers are given a sense of identity. ISIS is notorious for preying on young adults who lack direction in their lives and have no sense of purpose. As counterterrorism expert Richard Barrett put it, "The general picture provided by foreign fighters of their lives … suggests camaraderie, good morale and purposeful activity, all mixed in with a sense of understated heroism, designed to attract their friends."

By belonging and participating in ISIS-related activities, otherwise disillusioned teens believe they are making a positive difference in the world. According to researcher and journalist Lydia Wilson, participating in the cultivation of the Islamic State "gives one a sense of adventure, glory, and duty—a heady blend, especially for a young person who wishes to change the world." By exploiting the vulnerability of these teenagers, ISIS members are able to mold and form young people's thoughts and actions to their advantage, and even make them into war machines. Wilson says this lack of identity tactic often becomes "identity fusion" once new recruits become ingrained in the lifestyle of the Islamic State.

Identity fusion is the idea that an individual and the group they belong to have a shared identity, or essence. People with fused identities are more likely to die for the group's common cause, as they believe it gives the group strength. This may explain why otherwise normal people transform into suicide bombers without any indication that they would ever do such a thing.

The Women of ISIS

With the excessive use of weaponry and fighting presented online, it is no wonder that a large majority of recruits are males. However, females are continually joining ISIS too. As of 2015, nearly 10 percent of Western fighters in ISIS were women. Just like their male counterparts, their motivations for joining the Islamic state are varied in nature. The most cited reason stemmed from their religious beliefs. It was their intent to support the new caliphate and fulfill their religious duty as good Muslim women. This meant supporting their husbands who chose to join ISIS or marrying an established ISIS member. In addition, some women saw ISIS as an opportunity to build a new community. These women claim to have grown weary of the questionable morals of the Western world and looked toward this new society as a way to get back to the conservative Muslim ways in which they were raised. Conservative ideals also call for women to fill traditional roles, such as cooking, cleaning, and working in feminized career roles, such as nursing. These are seen as opportunities to support the Islamic State from the home, while the men go off and fight.

Dr. Mia Bloom explains that ISIS touts "a new kind of utopia." Dr. Bloom says that this "fantasy escape" convinces women that within ISIS "they will be empowered, have an exciting life, and do something meaningful with their lives." For men and women alike, the reasons for joining and promoting the Islamic State are expansive and varied. Some other reasons for joining the Islamic State include teenage rebellion, failed relationships, isolation, and need for adventure. It is obvious that ISIS has a mastery of social media and uses this to their advantage. With a combined use of propaganda and isolation techniques, recruiters are able to convince people to leave their lives and join their fight.

Living Within ISIS's Control

For the individuals who make it to ISIS-controlled territory without being arrested, their lives are changed forever. After being made promises of a new and exciting life, their expectations are often not met. As the accounts that follow explain, the Islamic State is far from the utopian society it strives to be. According to the International Center for the Study of Violent Extremism, "most [defectors] … tell stories of disillusionment and desperation, escape, and rejection of everything they saw in the so-called Islamic State."

Usaid Barho's Story

Usaid Barho was fourteen when he volunteered to be a suicide bomber for the Islamic State. Unlike other suicide bombers, he was unsuccessful in his mission. It was not faulty equipment, nor him being caught before he could detonate his vest that stopped Barho. Instead, he willingly exposed his vest of explosives to security personnel at the mosque in Baghdad he was set to attack—Barho was desperate to escape from ISIS. His journey had started after ISIS gained control of his Syrian town. They used the local mosque to teach anti-Shiite ideals and promote hate toward that particular faction of Muslims. Soon after, Usaid joined ISIS's ranks. As the *New York Times* explains, "he was brainwashed. But he admitted that he willingly ran away from home … and joined a training camp in the desert."

While completing his military training, Usaid began to question ISIS. "I noticed things I saw that were different from Islam." Smoking cigarettes had been a punishable offense in his home, yet he saw militants smoking within the camp. In addition, he said he witnessed militants engaging in sexual acts that ran counter to the Quran's teachings. Finally, the killing of innocent people did not sit well with Barho. He knew he had made a mistake in joining. In order to stand the best chance at defecting, he opted to become a suicide bomber. Barho figured this role would give him a better opportunity to escape without getting

Iraq's proximity to Syria explains why ISIS operates in both countries.

killed, and he was right. The officers who took him into custody even said, "if he was brought to court, we would be on his side, because he saved lives."

Syria and Umm Rashid

Not all teens who joined ISIS have stories with happy endings. Nor do they all necessarily start and end in Iraq. For many individuals affected by ISIS, Syria is often involved in some way. While it is true that the Islamic State came into existence within Iraq's borders, Syria also played a large part in the group's formation. Following al-Qaeda's denouncement of the group in 2014, in combination with the civil war that occupied the country in 2006 and 2007, ISIS was forced to look for resources outside of Iraq.

Syria was a logical choice for a few different reasons. First, it shared a border with Iraq, making it a strategic location for later military invasion. Second, a large area found in the north of Syria remained largely unoccupied, making it a good area for ISIS to regroup and remain unbothered. Third, Syria was experiencing similar government shortcomings that were comparable to what Iraq had experienced, making it a good place to find new recruits who wanted the chance at a better life than what their current government could provide. Lastly, establishing themselves in Syria would help fulfill one of the group's goals: to have a state that spanned the two countries.

When ISIS had reached a sustainable point in their recruitment numbers, they used that opportunity to begin the process of reclaiming the territory they had lost in Iraq. This started in June of 2014 with the capture of Mosul, Iraq's second largest city. As one soldier described the attack, "They took control of everything, and they are everywhere." In addition to Mosul, ISIS was also able to create a base in Aleppo, Syria. With their source of power coming from both Iraq and Syria, it is easy to see why it is common to hear about both countries when discussing ISIS. Beyond the shared borders, they also share similar stories of their victims, such as that of Umm Rashid.

Umm Rashid's story is quite different from Usaid Barho's. When she was younger, Rashid had dreams of being a doctor. However, when ISIS closed in, that dream took a back seat. As a young, single girl, she was at risk of being married off to a rebel militant or worse. In order to protect her from such a fate, Rashid's mother began looking for a suitable husband for her daughter. Coming from a very poor household, Rashid's options were limited. She ended up marrying her neighbor's son, Yusuf, when she was only fourteen. As Rashid explains, "My husband ... didn't have a say about what was going on at home. [His] sisters started to behave very badly toward me. My mother-in law beat me." After a few months, Yusuf ran away and found work with al-Nusra, a rival terrorist group. Money was plentiful again, and Rashid was showered in gifts. Then fighting broke out between al-Nusra and ISIS. Yusuf was wounded in battle and died from his injuries. After his death, Rashid's mother-in-law forced her from her house, saying "you brought bad luck to us." This was just the beginning of Rashid's descent into terrorism.

Rashid then lost both of her parents when a mortar shell landed on their home in 2014. Her sister lost her arm in the attack. Their house was decimated and now consisted of a single room. They had nothing. It was during this time that Rashid was befriended by a member of al-Khansaa, the female arm of the ISIS morality police. Umm al-Khattab helped Rashid and her sister by bringing them aid packages and meals whenever she could. Umm al-Khattab also found Rashid a new husband, who was a member of ISIS. He was rich and treated her well. He even allowed Rashid to bring her sister into his home, where she could still be cared for.

Shortly thereafter, Rashid joined Umm al-Khattab in al-Khansaa. Al-Khansaa had the power to fine, punish, and arrest people for any sort of morality offense. Rashid's particular brigade examined abayas in the marketplace. Abayas are robe-like dresses worn by Muslim women. Rashid and the brigade watched for abayas that were too transparent or tight. This sort of sexualized fashion was not to be worn by "good, Muslim women." Whenever they found someone breaking the morality laws in place they would

torture that woman so badly … she wouldn't be able to walk. Her husband needed to pay a fine and he needed to purchase the proper abaya and sign the paperwork that he would comply to the rules completely in the future. If the woman repeats her offense, we would take the husband and put him in a football field where coalition forces used to bomb a lot. We had a prison and we would put him in that prison. Most of the time he would die of fear because of the explosions in that field.

When asked if she felt bad about what she had done with her time in ISIS, Rashid showed little remorse. Instead, she said, "It made me strong! I would do the same thing again if given the opportunity. I escaped because I have a small child. I want to go back after the baby is grown." Unlike Usaid Barho, Rashid did not feel the same desire to escape from ISIS. Rather, she temporarily left since she could not perform the duties asked of her. For Rashid, ISIS meant an escape from her desperate situation and gave her a stable life with a rich husband. It also allowed her to be in a position of power, which was usually kept from women in the Middle East.

Alaa Abd al-Akeedi's Story

Unlike Usaid Barho and Umm Rashid, there are many instances of recruits who do not escape their duties and fulfill what is expected of them. Alaa Abd al-Akeedi's time with the Islamic State ended quite differently than Barho's or Rashid's. Having joined when he was around fifteen years of age, al-Akeedi was immediately placed in ISIS's militant training program to become a jihadist. According to a relative's interview with Reuters, al-Akeedi's father "was deeply distressed by his son's decision but feared punishment if he tried to remove him from [the] Islamic State's ranks." During his time with ISIS, the teen was isolated from family and friends and trained to believe in the extremist views of Islam that ISIS sets forth. In his final visit home, al-Akeedi informed his family that he was "going to seek martyrdom." They never saw him again.

In the months following that last visit, ISIS abandoned one of their posts in Mosul. A collection of letters meant for jihadists' families was found there. The letters were never mailed. In the pile was a letter from Alaa Abd al-Akeedi. It says, "My dear family, please forgive me … Don't be sad and don't wear the black clothes (of mourning). I asked to get married and you did not marry me off. So, by God, I will marry the seventy-two virgins in paradise [a common promise made to jihadists]." As his last words suggest, al-Akeedi genuinely believed that dying for ISIS's cause would bring him happiness in the afterlife.

More Stories of Escaping ISIS

With more and more people defecting from ISIS, outsiders often wonder how escape efforts are mounted. It should come as no surprise that leaving ISIS is not a simple task. ISIS's intent is that once a person joins their ranks, the recruit will live out their life attempting to establish the Islamic State. In order to return to their families and home countries, these individuals must choose between creating a well-thought-out plan to escape or simply running when the opportunity presents itself.

Others found people who were willing to smuggle them out of ISIS territory for a fee. As one former ISIS member recounts, "I was thinking all the time if they arrest me, if they stop me, they will behead me ... if you turn against ISIS, they will kill you." While there are many ways of attempting to leave ISIS, one thing is for sure. Individuals who are caught usually do not get another chance to escape. Those who are not executed immediately face execution at a later date or excruciating punishment upon return to ISIS territory.

Understanding ISIS Recruitment

ISIS recruiters are very good at what they do. By isolating individuals and promoting the Islamic State's way of life, they are able to convince people from a variety of countries to travel to the Middle East, as well as to carry out terrorist attacks in their respective countries. These recruits are often young and lack a sense of belonging or face unfortunate circumstances at home. Others yet are taken against their will and broken down in order to conform to ISIS's ideals.

Families run from war-torn Mosul in 2017.

CHAPTER FOUR

THE CASUALTIES OF ISIS

ISIS is responsible for hundreds of deaths across Iraq and the rest of the world. As of February 2017, ISIS has carried out or inspired 143 attacks in 29 different countries. These attacks have resulted in the deaths of 2,043 people. While these numbers are useful in quantifying casualties, they do little to elicit emotion for the lives lost. Each of those 2,043 people had a family, friends, and a day-to-day routine that likely resembles aspects of our own.

In addition to those who have died, there are many more people who live as ISIS's prisoners, never to be heard from again. These people and their stories are often lost in the mortar, rubble, and fear caused by ISIS.

The Fate of the Yazidi

Thousands of women have been forced to live out a life of slavery under ISIS's rule. Yazidi women are a primary target for enslavement by ISIS. Yazidis are among the oldest minority groups found in Iraq. They come from a predominantly Kurdish ethnic background. Yazidi people practice a religion different than most locals do, which takes on various aspects of Christianity and Islam. Because of this, they are targeted by the Islamic State, as well as al-Qaeda, for not holding "truly Islamic" beliefs and practicing heresy. Due to their devout practice, the seven hundred thousand Yazidis that are left face extermination. As their spiritual leader, Baba Sheikh explained,

> Seventy thousand people, or about fifteen percent of the Yazidi population in Iraq, fled the country. For a religion that does not accept converts and strongly discourages [marrying outside the faith], the assimilation of Yazidi youth in Europe threatens the faith's continued existence.

These traditions, in combination with the recent attacks on the population, mean that the Yazidi way of life may be entirely wiped out. Yazidis who are taken into ISIS custody often face death, men in particular. However, Yazidi men and women who have escaped describe conditions that may be a fate worse than death.

Yazidi Women

Yazidi women often experience an uncertain future of sex slavery, abuse, and forced marriage. Jihan, a Yazidi survivor, explains, "They put us in a filthy room and we all got sick … They told us that we would be sold, some as slaves, some as brides for the fighters." Most of the victims lose any hope for survival and even take comfort in the idea of death. One young girl named Nasima revealed that whenever an enemy plane flew over the place she was being held captive, she often hoped it would bomb them. At least then she would be put out of her misery, she thought. Rape was a common theme among captive Yazidi women. Many survivors describe a pattern of repeated sexual assault. Most Yazidi women tell only snippets

Many Yazidi women, like Jinan, pictured here, were subjects to unspeakable acts of torture and rape, simply because of their religious beliefs.

of what they faced at the hands of ISIS. However, one teenage victim was willing to share more of her story.

As a way to protect her family members that were still within ISIS custody, she refrained from giving her name. It all started when ISIS militants invaded Sinjar, in northwestern Iraq. Some of the townspeople fled; others were killed. Yet this fifteen-year-old girl and her two sisters were captured and were to be sold into "marriage." They were kept in a Badosh prison (located near Tal Afar) before being taken to Mosul, the location of ISIS's strongest base. From there, they were moved to Raqqa, Syria. Raqqa is where the majority of captured girls are brought to be sold.

The survivor was first sold to a Palestinian man. With the help of a disgruntled housekeeper, she was able to get her hands on a gun. She ultimately shot her captor and escaped. With nowhere to go, however, she returned to the original house where she and the other captured girls were kept in Raqqa. Unsurprisingly, the militants simply sold her again. This time she was sold to a Saudi militant. As she explains, "He told me, 'I'm going to change your name to Abeer, so your mother doesn't recognize you' ... 'You'll become Muslim, then I will marry you.'" She refused to let this happen. At one point, she noticed that some of the militants were taking a powdery drug. When no one was

Kurdish forces pushed ISIS out of Raqqa in 2017 but were left with a city reduced to rubble.

paying attention, she took some of this drug and mixed it in with their tea. They fell asleep soon after, and she fled.

After this escape, the survivor was able to convince someone to take her to her brother in Turkey, for a fee. They both returned to Iraq after being reunited. To this day, the whereabouts of her two sisters and other family members are unknown. Another teen, eighteen-year-old Maysa, was held by ISIS for nearly a year. She was first captured in Iraq and then taken to Syria. Maysa recalls that "one day we were able to arrange a rendezvous with my father at the Turkish border. [The man helping me] gave me his daughter's ID and drove me to the border where I was finally rescued."

Regardless of the particular details, all of the women who escaped seemed to tell different variations of the same story. According to the *Telegraph*, they "reported having seen dozens of other Yazidi women and children as young as five years old in captivity … and that they have relatives who are still missing." They, and many others, all faced much the same treatment: forced conversion to Islam, slavery, marriage, and rape. They had no idea what happened to their families and had no home to return to. Their identities as Yazidi people were all but left to the memories they had of the past. The Yazidi religion is not the only belief system that is targeted by ISIS, however.

Ismail's Story

Those who do not practice the Muslim religion are automatically targeted by Islamic State troops. When ISIS invaded Mosul, Iraq, in the summer of 2014, they were within range of one of the largest Christian groups in the country. Just east of Mosul is the town of Bartella. In this town, an excess of one hundred thousand Chaldean Catholics made their home. Upon ISIS's arrival, the people of Bartella were given a choice: either convert to Islam or pay ISIS for their safety. Most of the citizens instead opted to leave the region for sanctuary elsewhere in Kurdish regions of the country. Yet not everyone was able to make the journey. For

Ismail al-Kanon and his disabled mother, Jander, the trek was simply not an option. Ismail, who was only fourteen at the time, said, "We're the only ones who stayed, everybody else left. We had no clue what had happened." In an attempt to escape, the two hitched a ride, aiming to reach the capital of the Kurdish region of Iraq, Erbil. They did not make it. Halfway between Mosul and Erbil, they were stopped at a checkpoint that was manned by ISIS militants. When Ismail stated that he and his mother were Christians, they knocked him out. He was then tied up, along with his mother, and the two were taken to Mosul. Ismail and Jander would spend the next two years in ISIS custody.

Within the first few days of their capture, mother and son were forced to convert to Islam. Having come from a strongly devout Christian community, complete with six different churches, this was one of the hardest things Ismail had ever done. When presented with the option of conversion, Ismail's hesitation did not sit well with the ISIS guards. He recalls they "put the gun on my head and told my mother, 'If you don't convert we will kill your son.' We were scared. My mother told him to give us some time to think."

The militants agreed. However, during this time, they approached a captive in the cell next to Ismail and his mother's. This man was a devout Shiite Muslim. When he refused to convert, he was shot and killed on the spot. As

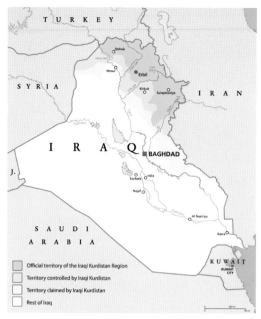

This map shows the Kurdish portions of Iraq in yellow.

a means of instilling fear in the pair, the militants then escorted Ismail and his mother over the man's corpse. The guard warned the two that this was the consequence of not converting. In order to survive, Ismail's mother convinced him to comply. Ismail recounts, "We told them yes, we will convert. They asked us to say the shahada, and we said it." (The shahada is the proclamation of Islam faith that is to be spoken by those converting to the religion.)

In a risky act of defiance, Ismail continued to wear a cross underneath his shirt even after he was converted. This would remain a symbol of his devotion to the Christian faith for the years following his capture. It served as a way for him to remember his true identity.

After being released from the ISIS prison, the pair were kept under a form of house arrest. Militants checked in on them and asked them to recite Muslim prayers. Any time Ismail and Jander answered militants' questions incorrectly, they were beaten. Ismail's mother had a more difficult time remembering things than Ismail did. As Ismail explains,

> *My mother is epileptic. She would learn something then forget it after she had a seizure. They would teach her, then come to her the next day, they would ask her the same question but she wouldn't know the answer.*

Because of his mother's difficulties, Ismail had to witness her being beaten and tortured many times. There was even a situation when the ISIS militants dug a needle into Jander's skin, causing her to bleed. They would take the needle out only when she answered their questions correctly. In addition to the torture, Ismail was faced with crippling isolation. He feared talking to anyone in case they discovered his Christian faith and turned him in. He spent his days playing video games and people-watching at the local market. When the ISIS members tired of torturing Ismail in his home, militants would arrest him and take him to prison for a few days at a time. While there, "they would give me twenty-five lashes, shave my head and then release me," he says. This was ISIS's way of breaking down Ismail's identity and reminding him that he was not in charge of his own future.

Ismail and Jander Escape

Knowing that their future was so uncertain, Ismail and his mother tried to escape many times. Every time they failed, they were beaten and returned to their guarded living quarters. Then one day, Ismail saw an opportunity that would eventually lead to a successful attempt. Having watched the news every day, Ismail was aware that there was an Iraqi-led offensive against ISIS in the works. When he finally felt that they had waited long enough, Ismail prepared his mother for their escape. The individuals guarding their living quarters were preoccupied with the approaching forces, so Ismail and Jander escaped to an apartment close to the front lines. When gunfire rang out from both sides, they ran. As Ismail explains,

> ISIS were on the roofs of the buildings, they saw us and started shooting at us. They aimed at my mother but [the bullet] went through her robe and didn't hit her. She could have died.

Even when faced with death, they still ran. With a makeshift white flag in hand, to symbolize their innocence, Ismail and his mother crossed into Iraqi coalition lines. When they arrived on the other side, they were liberated.

Mother and son were escorted to a refugee camp for a few days before going to Erbil, the capital of the Kurdish region. Of course, Ismail described himself as emotionally and physically tired by the whole ordeal. His Christian beliefs are also compromised because his "feelings towards ISIS are that I want to completely erase them. But at the same time our religion doesn't promote cruelty." While Bartella used to be his home, Ismail has no desire to return to the city. He concluded his story by saying that "I will leave Iraq ... it is ruined."

Cubs of the Caliphate

In the previous chapter, we considered cases of teens who voluntarily joined ISIS. Yet the terrorist group often gives young people no choice at all. When ISIS comes to a region, they tell young people that the only alternative to joining is death. Young soldiers are a crucial part of ISIS's strategy.

Referred to as the "Cubs of the Caliphate," young child soldiers are often stripped of their identities and indoctrinated to accept ISIS's views. Child soldiers are particularly valuable to terrorist organizations. Some child soldiers are placed on the front lines as suicide bombers. Terrorists find children useful in these situations because opposing forces are often unsure of whether the children are surrendering or pose a

REFUGEES OF ISIS

Because of the violence of ISIS, many people in Iraq are left without homes. With no place to go, these individuals and their families often end up in refugee camps. For some, that happens to be a camp found 12 miles (20 kilometers) outside of Mosul, while others are taken to Mazraa Base. This base is found near the village of Al-Mazraa, situated north of Baghdad. Tents line the streets of the camps, and each family gets one tent to call their own. After initial registration, the men are separated from the women and children for interrogation. Anxieties surrounding ISIS are high, and those running the camps want to ensure that they are not providing resources for a jihadist.

Life within refugee camps is defined by struggle. As one person explains, "In this remote, godforsaken patch of desert, camp residents are cut off from the world. There is no cell phone reception, no transportation, no electricity, no running water." Humanitarian efforts attempt to provide refugees with necessities like food and drinking water, though.

Few know what the future holds, so many refugees report appreciating the little things in the moment. For some, they will find extended family to move in with. Others still will be granted

Refugees cross into Turkey in 2014.

asylum from foreign countries and receive sponsorship. As for going back to their homes, CNN says, "even now, as Iraqi forces and their allies launch a major offensive to reclaim Mosul, the prospects of returning appear bleak." Everything is uncertain for these people, so they do the only thing they can do: wait.

threat. This allows children to get closer to targets than adult militants would, improving their chances of killing enemies upon detonation of their vests.

Children also prove to be more malleable. This means that ISIS can essentially convince them that radical Islam is the only way to live. Even after these children escape, this ideology is often so strongly ingrained in them that they pose threats for future generations. While these are only some of the so-called benefits of child soldiers, the effect on the children themselves is unimaginable. The stories coming from survivors are full of horrors that no child should ever have to face.

Thirteen-year-old Mohammed was told he could either join ISIS in their fight or face beheading. That's how he found himself at a training camp. As Mohammed explains, "For thirty days we woke up and jogged, had breakfast, then learned the Quran and the Hadith of the Prophet … Then we took courses on weapons, Kalashnikovs and other light military stuff." He was also not allowed to visit family or friends during this time. By isolating their "cubs," ISIS hopes to strip young people of their identities and force them to find comfort in the radicalized way of life that was presented to them. If they did not cooperate, Mohammed recalls various forms of abuse. In one case, he saw a "young

This ten-year-old boy was kidnapped by ISIS and forced to become a child soldier.

man who did not fast for Ramadan, so they crucified him for three days." In addition to beatings, children as young as five were witness to beheadings and even asked to kill prisoners themselves. If they refused, they received serious consequences and, in some cases, death.

In the words of Adiba Qasam, "Those kids are victims. They're under [ISIS] control." Qasam served as an activist for the children of ISIS and witnessed firsthand exactly what these children faced on a daily basis. As she explains,

> *Kids learn to tell time by reading clocks attached to timebombs. Arithmetic books teach kids addition and subtraction using pictures of bombs and AK-47s, alongside the traditional bananas and apples—making weapons of war seem like inane daily objects.*

Every single aspect of child soldiers' lives are designed to prepare them for war. They are led to believe their captors genuinely care for them. It is also standard for ISIS militants to train these children that their own parents are unbelievers, and therefore, deserve to die. One young militant, Zikran, was captured by ISIS when he was sixteen. In a short amount of time, he was indoctrinated into their way of thinking and unquestioningly followed what his captors said. He even recalls how eager his younger counterparts were to participate in jihad. CBS News reports that when teachers would come into Zikran's classroom and "ask who would want to go and explode themselves" the child would scream, "'We want to, we want to.'"

Those who escape are often further isolated from their communities due to their past. This only makes them more likely to return to their radical ways. By targeting the younger demographic, ISIS is planting the seed for future generations.

The Indirect Effects of ISIS

The Islamic State has had a very obvious effect on the country of Iraq and the regions around it. Their presence means daily bombings of cities, occupied areas falling under their control, and death for citizens. Beyond the individuals who are forced into slavery, imprisoned, or captured and trained as child soldiers, there are still those that experience indirect effects of the Islamic State and their activity in the Middle East. These are the political, social, and economic effects of ISIS in Iraq.

Political Effects

When it comes to the politics of Iraq, there have been a few key concerns that arise indirectly from ISIS. One of the most pressing is the officials that are being placed in office. According to World Bank and Transparency International, Iraq is the one hundred and seventieth most corrupt nation in the world. Remarkably, that designation was on a list of one hundred seventy-five countries total. That means there were only five countries considered more corrupt than Iraq. As one government official put it, "There is no solution. Everybody is corrupt, from the top of society to the bottom. Everyone. Including me." While there was corruption present before the Islamic State came to power, the terrorist group unquestionably provided greater opportunity for corrupt individuals to take advantage of the situation. With one of the largest public payrolls in the world, much of the corruption lies with public sector employees. Public sector employees account for nearly 33 percent of the Iraqi workforce, including military jobs. Finance minister Hoshyar Zebari says, "[The] biggest issue is ghost soldiers ... There are maybe $500–$600 million in salaries being paid to soldiers who don't exist. There are so many outlets for this money to go without any accountability."

Aside from people receiving the salaries of soldiers who do not exist, there are others still who pay their soldiers a percentage of their actual wages and pocket the rest. In addition, budgets are often blown out of proportion and call for more money than needed. For some corrupt officials, this is an opportunity to make even more money. By saying their budget for weapons is larger than it is, they are able to pocket the money that they do not use on weapons. Interestingly enough, money laundering is not solely a political issue. According to Mishan al-Jabouri, an Iraqi anti-corruption leader, "The problems here are social as much as everything. You are seen as weak if you don't steal. Everyone wants to claim power, because they know that nobody else is going to share power with them."

In an attempt to lessen the amount of corruption in government positions, Iraqi Prime Minister Haider al-Abadi introduced new legislation. Approved unanimously on August 11, 2015, this reform called for the elimination of multiple government offices. This included three vice presidents and a Deputy Prime Minister, and as many as 123 other officials. Some were corrupt individuals, such as Nouri al-Maliki, who nearly caused the country to erupt into civil war in

2013. Unfortunately, it also led to the dismissal of officials who were not corrupt, like Ayad Allawi, who was largely supported by the Sunni people. It was al-Abadi's hope that in eliminating these offices, he would lessen the corruption, as well as decrease the amount of financial burden placed on the Iraqi budget. Fewer people to pay meant less money to budget for.

However, due to the division between the Shia and Sunni sides of the government, in addition to lack of specific implementations and support, the Abadi reforms failed to make a difference. Officials' focus was placed on the current problem of the Islamic State, and Iraqi officials were not interested in focusing on internal problems.

Economic Effects

The Iraqi economy has also been crippled by ISIS. ISIS exerts outsize influence on oil production, a key part of Iraq's gross domestic product. In ISIS-controlled regions of ISIS, militants have destroyed and disrupted oil fields. In addition, these regions are often along established trade routes, thus stopping the flow of oil in and out of the country. According to the World Bank, "between May and July 2014, Iraq's exports declined by about 25 percent and its imports by 45 percent." Though these statistics were not caused by

ISIS alone, the other relevant factors are no comparison to the terrorist group's influence. Because of ISIS's interference in oil production, it is becoming increasingly obvious that Iraq lacks the economic diversity that helps to make other countries successful. According to Hoshyar Zebari,

> *We are 93 to 95 percent dependent on oil revenues ... We have exhausted our domestic borrowing ... We need to lose our dependability on oil. We need to prepare the public for change; on things such as VATs and other new measures. It is a question of a change in attitude. Here people are not accustomed to this.*

Of course, the issues Zebari raises affect many other aspects of the Iraqi economy as well.

One notable effect of Iraq's economic struggles is a weakened educational system within the country. The current state of Iraqi education stems from many problems. Not only does ISIS directly impact schools by bombing them, but they indirectly hinder students from learning for other reasons. With the nation's budget primarily focused on eradicating the Islamic State, there is little left to cover classroom renovation, or to even provide reliable roads and infrastructure surrounding schools. In addition,

TERROR ON THE TUBE

During the early hours of September 15, 2017, Londoners were just starting their commute to work. While some commuters drive, a majority rely on public transportation, such as the subway. Those boarding "the Tube" that morning were about to come face-to-face with terror. Around 8:20 a.m., a self-made bomb was detonated at the Parsons Green underground station. The attack left twenty-nine people injured, and ISIS claimed responsibility.

The attack, in combination with others around that time period, spurred action on United States soil. Using the attack to propel his legislation forward, President Donald Trump enacted a travel ban in the hopes of keeping the country safe. In a tweet, he said, "Making America safe is my number one priority. We will not admit those into our country we cannot safely vet." The president's plan called for a ban on travel to and from Syria and North Korea. Other countries, including Chad, Yemen, Libya, Somali, Iran, and Venezuela, had varying degrees of restrictions placed on them.

As Secretary of State Rex Tillerson put it, "the President is carrying out his duty to protect the American people." On the other hand, these travel restrictions make it impossible for innocent people and refugees from these areas to seek a safe space within United States borders.

the World Bank points out that it "is equally important to make sure that teachers are deployed and paid, textbooks are provided, language barriers are addressed, and security and safety of children are insured." Educational barriers further manifest due to the number of refugee and displaced children. Many of these children can no longer attend school because of ISIS's effects. On top of all that, there are fewer and fewer jobs for young people once they complete their schooling. Circumstances such as these give ISIS the leverage to seem like a viable option to young people in desperate situations.

Social Effects

The last area of Iraqi life that demonstrates ISIS's indirect effects is the social fabric of the nation. Because the Islamic State is fueled by the idea that the Shiite Muslims are lesser than the Sunni faction, these ideas have found their way into everyday life. Some communities continue to ostracize minorities, and groups and individuals cause civil unrest. In combination with the stagnant economy and divided politics, those who join ISIS but end up escaping continue to perpetuate the terrorist group's ideals. This puts Iraq at risk for future development of another terrorist group that shares the same beliefs as ISIS does but has learned from their mistakes.

Many Victims, Many Survivors

The effects of the Islamic State can be seen in nearly every aspect of Iraqi life. While some effects are more obvious than others, the vast majority of its citizens have had their lives changed in one way or another. The Yazidi people are now faced with the possibility of extinction, with their men being brutally murdered, women being taken for sex slaves, and children being used as pawns by militants. For Christians and adherents of religions outside of Islam, life is lived in a constant state of fear. Furthermore, ISIS routinely targets young people, whom they force to fight using threats of death.

These are only some of the effects of ISIS, and they only scratch the surface. Beyond the obvious, ISIS continues to impact the Iraqi economy by barricading access to oil, blocking trade routes, and limiting resources. In addition, the Islamic State has had a divisive effect on the government of Iraq. The terrorist group's presence has only worsened corruption and inefficiency. This, in turn, has prevented young people from receiving proper schooling, which only makes them more likely to join terror groups like ISIS. It all seems like an unending, hopeless cycle. However, there is good news coming out of Iraq: ISIS is losing their hold.

Iraqi soldiers work to eradicate ISIS in the desert bordering Syria in 2017.

CHAPTER FIVE

SOLVING TERROR IN IRAQ

There is no question that ISIS has had an impact across the globe. From terrorist attacks in the United States, France, England, and many other countries, to recorded executions of captives, it's difficult to think of a region that's avoided the violence. In Iraq, the terror group instills fear and commits atrocities and murder. Yet there are actions that can be taken by the global community to stop ISIS. And it's not just military campaigns or new legislation that makes a difference—even everyday people can help in the fight against ISIS.

What Can Be Done?

Eradicating ISIS requires taking away their resources. ISIS's efforts rely on their access to large sums of money. That's where oil fields come into play. According to *Time*, the "daily revenue from ISIS oil production lies between one and three million dollars a day." With such a large daily influx of cash, they are able to feed and provide for the soldiers, and their families, that support and fight for the Islamic State and their cause. Additionally, they use this revenue to buy weapons and purchase other resources. They even use the oil itself in their vehicles. It might seem strange to buy oil from a terrorist, but such a purchase can offer a few key benefits to its buyers. Since ISIS-made crude oil does not have to follow certain regulations or taxation, ISIS can "sell both crude oil and refined products through well-established smuggling networks" at a cheaper price than the normal market value, *Time* reports.

In addition to oil, the land ISIS controls is where a sizeable amount of the nation's wheat is grown. Just like the oil fields, these wheat fields benefit the civilians within ISIS as well as provide another opportunity for commerce on black markets. Since the Islamic State gains so much from the land within its control, focusing on regaining ground has the potential to hobble ISIS. With the help of American,

ISIS continues to control important land in Iraq, including portions of the country where wheat grows.

Iraqi, Kurdish, and Syrian troops, land has been reclaimed in different regions. According to an International Energy Agency report from 2014, "the aerial campaign has brought ISIS oil production down to around twenty thousand barrels per day, from a high of around seventy thousand a couple of months ago."

While there is more land to recover, there are already signs ISIS is weakening. Without the money to provide for their people, more and more recruits will defect. Less money also equates to less weaponry. A weakened ISIS military will allow for more successful antiterrorism campaigns. Lastly, in taking back the land that ISIS occupies, the group would have fewer Iraqi civilians under their control. Without the available resources and people to extort, ISIS would take a huge financial hit and lose a large amount of the progress

THE MENTAL HEALTH OF TEENS IN A TIME OF TERROR

For teens in war-torn areas, young adulthood is no time for play. During a critical time of development, minors in parts of Iraq and Syria are exposed to war and death everywhere they look. This has a wide variety of impacts on their mental health.

For many, experiencing mental issues such as post-traumatic stress disorder and "toxic stress" (when the mind is always in "fight or flight" mode) is not uncommon. For those displaced from Mosul, mental health professionals have been able to see the effects firsthand. As psychologist Dr. Marcia Brophy of Save the Children International explains, "[The children I met] rarely even smiled. It was as though they lost the ability to be children." Because of the emotional stress that ISIS has caused, children across Iraq will need the support of mental health professionals into their adulthood. Of the children Brophy spoke to, nearly 90 percent had lost a family member, with some even seeing them killed. When asked to play a game that would make certain things disappear, Iraqi children chose things such as "war" and "sadness." In comparison, British children responded with foods they did not like. Even after the threat of ISIS has been neutralized, its effects will be felt by those who survived for a long time to come.

they have made. As more people left ISIS, the cycle would continue until ISIS has nothing left.

The next important part of antiterrorism strategy involves the upper ranks of the Islamic State. This includes leaders, department heads, and high-ranking military officers. These are the people that determine the group's strategic moves, make orders, and set ISIS's agenda. By targeting and killing these leaders, the group as a whole loses direction. This was seen in the effort to dismantle al-Qaeda. As previously mentioned, once Osama bin Laden was removed from power, the terrorist group rapidly lost its hold. While al-Qaeda is still around today, they are nowhere near the same powerful threat as they were in their prime, and they continue to lose top leaders to airstrikes and military encounters. This same tactic can be applied to ISIS. By eliminating those in charge, the group will become easy to divide. Upon capture, high-ranking officials could be used to provide useful information, such as the locations of Islamic State factions found outside of the Middle East. As terrorist attacks in England and France suggest, such branches of ISIS are a very real threat. Beyond removing ISIS's key leaders, cutting off their resources, and making gains on the ground, there is one other key area to weaken their reach.

Fighting Tech with Tech

Unlike the terrorist groups that came before them, the Islamic State developed during an era of rapid technological innovation. This gave them a number of advantages, including the ability to connect with people all over the world. In fact, one of the most important indicators of their success is how effectively ISIS reached the masses through social media. In an op-ed, journalists Tara Mooney and Andrew Byers state that it's time to think beyond typical military force:

> To defeat ISIS, we need an entirely new strategy, one that takes on ISIS where it is highly effective—in cyberspace.
>
> While ISIS continues to foment regional instability in the greater Middle East, its prowess online has made it a threat to Western nations, as well. ISIS focuses significant resources on cyberspace, where it has a global presence, using sophisticated techniques to electronically communicate with its far-flung sympathizers, spread its propaganda and recruit operatives around the world ...
>
> To defeat ISIS in cyberspace, the United States must first commit itself to establishing a strategic

plan that emphasizes flexibility, adaptability, information-sharing and cooperation among government agencies. We must create cyber-teams as flexible and adaptable as the terrorists they are fighting.

We must maintain continuous, systematic monitoring of all of ISIS's online activities, and create new online content quickly. ISIS's patterns of propaganda dissemination are evolving but predictable, based on trial and error. Our current efforts create a series of reactive, mostly ineffective, counter-narratives that potential jihadis readily dismiss.

Considering that the Islamic State has a large presence and following online, it would make sense to make more effective attacks on their social media campaigns. ISIS uses social media for many things, including attracting followers to the Middle East, communicating with sympathizers, coordinating attacks across the globe, and controlling the narrative surrounding their recorded executions and kidnappings. While an online presence does not provide the same monetary gain that their land holdings do, some experts argue that what it does provide is far more valuable

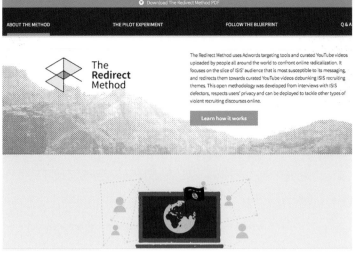

The
Redirect
Method

The Redirect Method uses Adwords targeting tools and curated YouTube videos uploaded by people all around the world to confront online radicalization. It focuses on the slice of ISIS' audience that is most susceptible to its messaging, and redirects them towards curated YouTube videos debunking ISIS recruiting themes. This open methodology was developed from interviews with ISIS defectors, respects users' privacy and can be deployed to tackle other types of violent recruiting discourses online.

Learn how it works

The Redirect Method lessens ISIS's internet recruiting power.

than oil. With this in mind, there are many existing solutions in place that attempt to minimize ISIS's web presence.

As it stands, there are two facets to the issue. One is how to prevent people from falling victim to Islamic State recruiters to begin with. The other asks how a recruiter's efforts can be thwarted before attracting the attention of ISIS sympathizers. This first idea of prevention has become a talking point within the walls of one of the internet's most important companies: Google. Known as the Redirect Method, Google's anti-ISIS tactic "at its heart [is] a targeted advertising campaign: let's take these individuals who are vulnerable to ISIS's recruitment messaging and instead show them information that refutes it," says Yasmin Green, the head of research and development for Jigsaw, Google's think-tank.

A Closer Look at the Redirect Method

The Redirect Method works much the same way as Google Adwords. Google Adwords recognizes certain words in a person's search and then tailors the ads that appear within the browser to match what he or she was searching for. With the Redirect Method, Google picks out search words that are popular among ISIS recruits and then returns results that expose these potential recruits to the negative side of ISIS in an effort to dissuade them from joining.

The Redirect Method is an innovation of Jigsaw. The plan hopes to catch those who are most likely to fall victim to recruitment efforts. The unpleasant sides of ISIS returned by the method include "clips like testimonials from former extremists, imams denouncing ISIS's corruption of Islam, and surreptitiously filmed clips inside the group's dysfunctional caliphate," according to *Wired*. This all sounds great, but does it actually work? In the words of tech analysts with Jigsaw:

> *Over the course of about two months, more than three hundred thousand people were drawn to the anti-ISIS YouTube channels. Searchers actually clicked on Jigsaw's three or four times more often than a typical ad campaign.*

Jigsaw's efforts have been so successful that the tech giant hopes to apply this method to other groups, such as other terrorist organizations and white supremacists. Aside from crippling their online presence, there are small everyday things that can be done to aid in the fight against ISIS as well.

Pens Before Swords

Education can have a large impact on the Islamic State. Muslims and non-Muslims alike can weaken ISIS by learning more about the religion of Islam. Even though ISIS brands itself as being a religious group, the radicalized views they take are not backed up by their religious texts. While ISIS cites passages about violence and jihad to use from the Quran, there are equally as many passages about peace and harmony. Had some of the recruited Muslims that were recruited known more about Islam, perhaps their devoutness to their religion would have pointed them in a different direction. As for non-Muslims, knowing more about the faith can have a few key effects in the global community. The first is that a certain level of understanding can make tangible differences at home. Many people wrongfully assume that the Muslims supporting ISIS are similar to the Muslims attending mosque services up the road from their house. Differentiating between the two creates acceptance—and safer communities for Muslims.

TEEN ACTIVISM IN IRAQ

Among the bombs and gunfire, there are individuals fighting back against ISIS in nonviolent ways. One such person is eighteen-year-old Nenous Thabit. This teen activist uses his artistic ability to drive out the hate that ISIS promotes. When the Islamic State entered his home city of Nimrud, they began destroying sculptures, murals, and other centuries-old artifacts. ISIS believed that these pieces of art served as idols, which are strictly forbidden in the Muslim religion. In the wake of the tragedy, Thabit took it upon himself to re-create some of these pieces, which he believed to be the work of his ancestors. As he puts it, "they waged a war on art and culture, so I decided to fight them with art." While Thabit is not out actively fighting against ISIS, practicing art puts him in danger too. Thabit explains that "in Iraq, there are people who are killed because they are sculptors ... ISIS view[s] them as apostate. So continuing to sculpt is a message that we will not be intimidated by those devils." When he initially started the project, Thabit completed eighteen statues and a mural in the course of a year. Before the ISIS attack, Thabit just practiced sculpting in his free time. Having been trained by his father from the age of seven, working with clay and other malleable materials has been part of his life for a long time. It is Thabit's hope to further his studies and attend an art school when he graduates from high school.

Education Is the Way Forward

Outside of learning about Islam, even attending basic school classes can help in the fight against ISIS. For many children, ISIS has disrupted their ability to attend school. In areas that are at risk of an attack, children and teenagers are often sent on holidays. While this ensures that each child will likely be with their family in the case of an attack, it also prevents them from learning and forming plans for their future. For children living in Hasensham Camp, they are combating the extremist group by pursuing their education, regardless of the risks. When they arrive at the refugee camp, "going back to school is one of the only returns to normality for children displaced by ISIS." Some children are as many as three grades behind. But instead of giving up on their education, they show enthusiasm and eagerness when given the opportunity to catch up. For thirteen-year-old Zahra, school is a prominent path into the future. As she explains, "ISIS made us leave school. Going back is our revenge against them. I'm going to be a doctor." For those that are trapped within ISIS-controlled areas, they are not given the same luxury. According to the *Independent*:

> *When the militants seized new towns they either took over or closed all schools under their control, implementing their own curriculum.*

Mathematics textbooks used sums such as "bomb plus gun equals …" to indoctrinate children from a young age, causing many parents to pull their children out to avoid the extremist influences altogether.

Education will come to influence ISIS either negatively or positively in the coming years, depending on the development of replacement programs within Iraq. The sooner Iraqi children are able to return to school, the better. Without education, children are given little hope for the future. Without a way to benefit their community and support themselves, many will fall into the same traps that their older peers did: ISIS recruitment. Recruits are typically those who are not well off in their current living situation, which is what ISIS hopes to create by destroying schools across the country. In this seemingly endless cycle, the only solution is to adequately educate the children of Iraq.

Building Strong Communities

Outside of understanding what Islam is—and isn't, there are two more strategies that can be used to limit the Islamic State's appeal. It has been documented that the majority of ISIS recruits are people who lacked a sense of belonging within their communities. This "lone wolf" mentality is seen in many people who act out in violent ways. ISIS recruiters play into this sense of isolation by convincing recruits that no one understands them. This tactic makes people much more likely to join a group such as ISIS. By recognizing people who appear isolated and reaching out to them, it is possible to build stronger communities and ensure that no

The Jalil Khayat Mosque in Erbil

one is an easy target for ISIS's lies. In addition to loners, ISIS goes after individuals who are in desperate situations. People who are jobless, homeless, or otherwise going through a rough patch in life are prime targets in the eyes of ISIS. The Islamic State pulls desperate people in with promises of honor and money, which make it hard for people to say no. Here again, strong communities can make a difference. It turns out that a simple act of kindness can go a long way in the fight against terrorism.

A Hopeful Future

There are many different ways to combat terrorism. On the global front, many countries are enacting pieces of legislation to quell terrorist activities. In addition, there are strategic plans in place to choke ISIS of its available resources. By taking back the land they have come to control, ISIS stands to lose its revenue streams: the oil fields, agricultural industry, and extortion money from the people living there. As of November 2017, a coalition and Iraqi troops took back ISIS's last town in Iraq, Rawah. Though ISIS still holds scraps of land in the nation, it was a major victory. And that victory seems to be a harbinger of good things to come.

Governments are also working to locate key leaders within ISIS. Capturing or targeting these leaders could lead to the fall of the caliphate. Beyond physical combat, there are methods in place to stop ISIS and its presence online and in person.

The rise of ISIS is a complex story. With ISIS's founder learning from al-Qaeda and then forging his own generation of terror, it's no wonder that al-Zarqawi's death in 2006 was not enough to stop the group's growth. Yet beyond all the violence, it is not a hopeless battle

Soldiers hold a burned ISIS flag after a successful military campaign against the group.

against ISIS. Many steps are being taken to weaken the terrorist group. By working together, the global community can ensure that ISIS is eradicated once and for all.

CHRONOLOGY

1920   The modern nation of Iraq is formed.

1932   Iraq achieves independence from Great Britain.

2004   Abu Musab al-Zarqawi forms al-Qaeda in Iraq.

2006   Following Zarqawi's death, Abu Ayyub al-Masri announces the formation of the Islamic State in Iraq.

2007   ISIS is pushed out of the Iraqi capital of Baghdad. Membership dwindles among the terrorist group.

2009   Prime Minister Maliki targets Sunni leaders, creating separatist tendencies that positively impact ISIS numbers.

2010   Abu Bakr al-Baghdadi becomes the leader of the Islamic State after Abu Omar al-Baghdadi and Abu Ayyub al-Masri are killed.

2014   ISIS overtakes Raqqa and makes it their capital; al-Qaeda cuts ties with ISIS.

2017   ISIS loses its hold on Rawah. It is the last town under the terror group's control in Iraq.

GLOSSARY

apostate Someone who purposefully goes against a religious belief or principle.

caliphate The area controlled or ruled by a caliph, or Muslim leader.

coalition A partnership or temporary alliance with a common goal.

coup A sudden, violent, and illegal seizure of power from a government.

Daesh An acronym representing the Arabic name for the Islamic State (al-Dawla al-Islamiya fi al-Iraq wa al-Sham).

demographics The ways in which a given population can be broken into particular groups, such as by age, race, or gender.

detonate To ignite, or cause to explode.

disillusionment To discover that something is not as good as previously thought.

doxing The act of finding information about a targeted person and purposefully exposing it.

exodus When a large group of people leave an area.

extort To force or threaten someone into doing something.

federal parliamentary representative democratic republic
A combination of a federal republic and a parliamentary republic. It is made up of states that rely on parliaments to make decisions.

grooming Training someone for a particular purpose.

hacktivists A computer hacker who hacks for the greater good.

humanitarian efforts Material or other assistance aimed at saving lives and alleviating suffering.

infrastructure The most basic physical structures and facilities, like buildings and roads.

jihadists Fighters against "enemies" of Islam.

Kurdish people An ethnic group found in the Middle East; also known as Kurds.

mortar A device used to shoot bombs at high angles.

propaganda Materials used to promote a particular point of view that are typically biased and misleading.

regime An authoritarian form of government, often military in nature.

FURTHER INFORMATION

Books

Gerges, Fawaz A. *ISIS: A History.* Princeton, NJ: Princeton
University Press: 2016.

IraqiGirl. *IraqiGirl: Diary of a Teenage Girl in Iraq.* Chicago:
Haymarket Books, 2009.

McCants, William. *The ISIS Apocalypse: The History,
Strategy, and Doomsday Vision of the Islamic State.*
New York: St. Martin's Press, 2015.

Warrick, Joby. *Black Flags: The Rise of ISIS.* New York:
Anchor Books, 2015.

Websites

UNICEF Iraq

https://www.unicef.org/iraq/

Find news and firsthand accounts from Iraqis on
UNICEF's site.

**United States Department of Defense:
Operation Inherent Resolve**

https://www.defense.gov/OIR/

This website is dedicated to the United States's progress in
the fight against ISIS, in an operation known as "Operation

Inherent Resolve." The Department of Defense posts articles, information about airstrikes, and more.

United States Department of State: Global Coalition to Defeat ISIS

https://www.state.gov/s/seci/

Run by the United States government, this website includes fact sheets, press releases, and blog posts related to the fight against ISIS.

Videos

"In the fight against ISIS, Kurds seek chance to govern themselves"

https://www.youtube.com/watch?v=IEw5FQaK0pI

PBS NewsHour provides a look at the circumstances Kurds face in war-torn Iraq.

"ISIS fighters' families await their fate in a refugee camp in Iraq"

https://www.youtube.com/watch?v=T-7Bhm68IJU

Interviews with women in a refugee camp in Iraq reveal just how complicated it will be to move past war and conflict.

BIBLIOGRAPHY

Al-Salhy, Suadad, and Tim Arango. "Sunni Militants Drive
    Iraqi Army Out of Mosul." *New York Times,* June 10,
    2014. https://www.nytimes.com/2014/06/11/world/
    middleeast/militants-in-mosul.html.

Arango, Tim. "A Boy in ISIS. A Suicide Vest. A Hope to
    Live." *New York Times*, December 26, 2014. https://
    www.nytimes.com/2014/12/27/world/middleeast/syria-
    isis-recruits-teenagers-as-suicide-bombers.html.

Berlinger, Joshua. "ISIS' child soldiers: What will happen
    to 'cubs of the caliphate'?" CNN, May 28, 2015. http://
    www.cnn.com/2015/05/20/middleeast/isis-child-
    soldiers/index.html.

Blaker, Lisa. "The Islamic State's Use of Online Social
    Media." *Military Cyber Affairs 1,* no. 1 (2015).
    doi:10.5038/2378-0789.1.1.1004.

CBS News and the Associated Press. "Young girl snatched
    by ISIS tells of her escape." October 11, 2014. https://
    www.cbsnews.com/news/isis-victim-tells-her-story-of-
    captivity-escape-from-militant-group/.

Chulov, Martin. "Post-war Iraq: 'Everybody is corrupt, from top to bottom. Including me.'" *Guardian*, February 19, 2016. https://www.theguardian.com/world/2016/feb/19/post-war-iraq-corruption-oil-prices-revenues.

CNN Staff. "Timeline: Osama bin Laden, over the years." CNN, May 2, 2011. http://www.cnn.com/2011/WORLD/asiapcf/05/02/bin.laden.timeline/index.html.

Cordesman, Anthony H. *Iraqi Stability and the "ISIS War."* PDF. Center for Strategic & International Studies, August 12, 2015.

D'Agata, Charlie. "How ISIS-trained child soldiers are a ticking time bomb." CBS News, July 29, 2017. https://www.cbsnews.com/news/isis-trained-child-soldiers-cbsn-on-assignment/.

Di Giovanni, Janine, Leah McGrath Goodman, and Damien Sharkov. "How Does ISIS Fund Its Reign of Terror?" *Newsweek,* March 5, 2016. http://www.newsweek.com/2014/11/14/how-does-isis-fund-its-reign-terror-282607.html.

Froelich, Amanda. "This Teen Is Re-Creating Sculptures That Were Destroyed By ISIS." True Activist, November 22, 2016. http://www.trueactivist.com/this-teen-is-re-creating-sculptures-that-were-destroyed-by-isis/.

Greene, Richard Allen, and Nick Thompson. "ISIS: Everything You Need to Know." CNN, August 11, 2016. http://www. cnn.com/2015/01/14/world/isis-everything-you-need-to-know/index.html.

"Iraqi PM Abadi Removes 123 Officials Amid Reform Drive." Deutsche Welle, September 9, 2015. http://www.dw.com/en/iraqi-pm-abadi-removes-123-officials-amid-reform-drive/a-18704538.

Jarrett, Laura, and Sophie Tatum. "Trump Administration Announces New Travel Restrictions." CNN, September 25, 2017. http://www.cnn.com/2017/09/24/politics/trump-travel-restrictions/index.html.

Kenworthy, Josh. "Getting out of ISIS: American Man among the Few to Escape." *Christian Science Monitor,* March 18, 2016. https://www.csmonitor.com/World/Middle-East/2016/0318/Getting-out-of-ISIS-American-man-among-the-few-to-escape.

Lister, Tim, and Ray Sanchez, Mark Bixler, Sean O'Key, Michael Hogenmiller and Mohammed Tawfeeq. "ISIS goes global: 143 Attacks in 29 Countries Have Killed 2,043." CNN, February 13, 2017. http://www.cnn.com/2015/12/17/world/mapping-isis-attacks-around-the-world/index.html.

McCants, William. "Who Is Islamic State Leader Abu Bakr al-Baghdadi?" BBC News, March 8, 2016. http://www. bbc.com/news/world-middle-east-35694311.

———. *The ISIS Apocalypse: The History, Strategy, and Doomsday Vision of the Islamic State.* New York: St. Martins Press, 2016.

McKernan, Bethan. "'School is our revenge on Isis': Children fight extremism with education in Iraq." *Independent,* May 12, 2017. http://www.independent. co.uk/news/world/middle-east/mosul-isis-battle-latest-children-refugees-displaced-fighting-education-school-idp-camps-unicef-a7733366.html.

Pariona, Amber. "Leading Countries Growing Dates (Fresh Date Palm Fruits)." WorldAtlas, August 29, 2016. http:// www.worldatlas.com/articles/world-leading-countries-growing-fresh-dates.html.

Patton, Mike. "The Five Highest Unemployment Rates in the World." *Forbes,* December 28, 2015. https:// www.forbes.com/sites/mikepatton/2015/12/28/ the-five-highest-unemployment-rates-in-the-world/#7b58eca640a5.

Peresin, Anita. "Fatal Attraction: Western Muslims and ISIS." *Perspectives on Terrorism* 9, no. 3. Retrieved September 25, 2017. http://www.terrorismanalysts.com/ pt/index.php/pot/article/view/427/html.

Schwartz, Zach. "We Asked an Iraqi Teen What She Thinks of ISIS and America." *Vice,* August 29, 2014. https://www.vice.com/en_au/article/av4ygk/we-asked-an-iraqi-teen-what-she-thinks-of-isis-and-america-829.

Sly, Liz. "Al-Qaeda disavows any ties with radical Islamist ISIS group in Syria, Iraq." *Washington Post,* February 3, 2014. https://www.washingtonpost.com/world/middle_east/al-qaeda-disavows-any-ties-with-radical-islamist-isis-group-in-syria-iraq/2014/02/03/2c9afc3a-8cef-11e3-98ab-fe5228217bd1_story.html?utm_term=.1c60c79fa9b0.

Spero, Domani. "State Dept's Antiterrorism Assistance Program Costs Approx $1,800/Student Per Day of Training." Diplopundit, April 4, 2013. https://diplopundit.net/2012/05/30/state-depts-antiterrorism-assistance-program-costs-approx-1800student-per-day-of-training/.

Titus, Mandi. "The Weather & Climate of Iraq in 2017." *USA Today*, retrieved September 10, 2017. http://traveltips.usatoday.com/weather-climate-iraq-50023.html.

Tomlinson, Lucas. "Size of ISIS army 'remains the same' since last year, US official says." Fox News, February 4, 2016. http://www.foxnews.com/politics/2016/02/04/size-isis-army-remains-same-since-last-year-us-official-says.html.

Wilcock, David. "Iraqi children suffering from 'toxic stress' after fleeing Mosul as war on ISIS rages around them." *Mirror*, July 5, 2017. http://www.mirror.co.uk/news/world-news/iraqi-children-suffering-toxic-stress-10739308.

Wilson Center. "Timeline: the Rise, Spread and Fall of the Islamic State." July 19, 2016. https://www.wilsoncenter.org/article/timeline-rise-and-spread-the-islamic-state.

Wilson, Lydia. "Understanding the Appeal of ISIS." *New England Journal of Public Policy* 29, no. 1 (March 20, 2017).

Yayla, Anne Speckhard Ahmet. "Making a Monster: How I Became an ISIS Bride." *Daily Beast*, August 31, 2017. https://www.thedailybeast.com/bride-of-isis-the-making-of-a-monsterpart-i.

INDEX

Page numbers in **boldface**
are illustrations

al-Khansaa, 53–54
al-Qaeda, 12–13, 16, 21–27,
    29, 32–33, 40–41, 51,
    60, 87, 97
al-Qaeda in Iraq (AQI), 26
Anonymous (activist group),
    45
Antiterrorism Assistance
    Program (ATA), 19
apostate, 93

Baghdad, 6, **8**, 16, **20**, 25,
    31, 34–35, 50, 70
Baghdadi, Abu Bakr, 16–17,
    16, 29
Baghdadi, Abu Omar, 26–29
bin Laden, Osama, 22–23,
    25–26, 29, 33, 87

caliphate, 27, 48, 69, 91, 97
child soldiers, 69, 72, **73**, 74
Christians, 60, 64–67, 69, 81

coalition, 14–15, 54, 68, 97
corruption, 11, 75–77, 81, 91
coup, 9

Daesh, 12, 14
demographics, 38, 47, 74
detonate, 50, 79
disillusionment, 50
doxing, 45

education, 78, 80, 92, 94-95
exodus, 11–12
extort, 13, 18, 85, 97

Facebook, 41, 43
federal parliamentary
    representative
    democratic republic, 10
forced conversion, 64–66
forced marriage, 18, 61–62,
    64

Global Coalition Against
    ISIS, 14–15
Google, 90–91

grooming, 39

hacktivists, 45
House of Wisdom, the, 6
humanitarian efforts, 70

infrastructure, 15, 19, 78
Islam, 23–24, 37, 46, 50,
    56, 60, 64–66, 72, 81,
    91–92, 94–95
Islamic Golden Age, 5–6
Islamic State, 7, 12, 21,
    26–29, 32, 38–39, 42,
    47–51, 55–57, 60, 64,
    74–75, 77–78, 80–81,
    84, 87–90, 92–93, 95–96
isolation, 42, 49, 67, 96
Israel, 7–8

jihadists, 24–25, 39, 44,
    55–56, 70

Kurdish people, 7–9, 11, 60,
    64–65, **66**, 69, 85

Libya, 13, 19, 79

Masri, Abu Ayyub, 26, 29
Middle East, 10, 12–14, 24,
    26, 39, 41, 43, 55, 57,
    75, 87–89
mortar, 53, 59
Mosul, 30, 32, **33**, 52, 56,
    62, 64–65, 70–71, 86
Muslim, 11, 15, 22, 25, 42,
    44, 46–48, 54, 62, 64,
    66, 92–93

oil, 10–11, 13–14, 77–78, 81,
    84–85, 90, 97

Pakistan, 19, 33
propaganda, 41, 44, 46, **46**,
    49, 88–89

radical, 15, 24–25, 39,
    43–44, 72, 74, 92
recruitment, 14, 28, 37–40,
    44–45, 52, 57, 90–91, 95
Redirect Method, 90–91, **90**
refugee camps, 69–70, 94
regime, 25

Shiite Muslim, 11, 24–26, 50,
    65, 80
social media, 38–39, **40**,
    41–43, 45–46, 49, 88–89
Sunni Muslim, 11, 16, 23,
    25–26, 28, 77, 80
Syria, 7, 12–14, 32, 50–52,
    51, 62–63, 79, 85–86

Taliban, 24
Twitter, 38, 41, 43, 45

Yazidi, 18, 60–61, 64, 81

Zarqawi, Abu Musab, 12,
    22–26, 97
Zawahiri, Ayman, 29

ABOUT THE AUTHOR

Ashley M. Ehman is the author of *The Power of C++*. She is a graduate of Carroll University, where she double-majored in information technology and professional writing, with an emphasis in graphic design. She currently lives in Madison, Wisconsin. Feel free to visit her portfolio at: https:// ashleyehman.wordpress.com/.